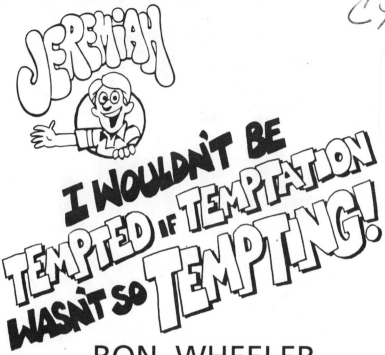

JEREMIAH

I WOULDN'T BE TEMPTED IF TEMPTATION WASN'T SO TEMPTING!

RON WHEELER

 BEACON HILL PRESS OF KANSAS CITY

KANSAS CITY, MISSOURI

THE ADVENTURES OF...

JEREMIAH

by ©1988
Roy Wheeler
H-10

JEREMIAH COMES TO MATT WITH A REQUEST THIS SUNDAY MORNING.

WHAT'S UP?

COME ON, MATT, GIVE US A HAND.

THEY'RE SHORT A COUPLE USHERS FOR THE OFFERING HERE!

USHERING?

I DON'T WANT TO USHER.

QUIT COMPLAINING AND GET ON THE OTHER SIDE OF THIS AISLE.

MATT AND JEREMIAH MUDDLE THROUGH THE COLLECTION...

...AND ONLY ONCE DO THEY PASS IT DOWN THE SAME ROW TWICE.

WE GAVE ALREADY.

OOPS! SORRY!

WOW! WHAT DO WE DO WITH ALL THIS LOOT, JEREMIAH?

THE ADVENTURES OF... JEREMIAH

by ©1988 Roy Wheeler H-11

LATE SUNDAY, MATT APPROACHES JEREMIAH.

SAY, JEREMIAH, REMEMBER WHEN WE WERE USHERING TODAY?

YEAH?

WELL, I LEFT MY BIBLE IN THE CHURCH OFFICE WHEN WE WERE DROPPING OFF THE OFFERING.

SO?

WELL YOU'VE GOT A KEY TO THAT OFFICE, DON'T YOU?

YEAH, THEY GAVE ME A KEY SO I COULD GET YOUTH MINISTRY SUPPLIES.

BUT WHY DON'T YOU JUST WAIT AND GET YOUR BIBLE TOMORROW WHEN THE OFFICE IS OPEN?

OH, I COULDN'T DO THAT.

WHAT WOULD I DO FOR MY PERSONAL DEVOTIONS TONIGHT?

YOU WOULDN'T WANT ME TO GO TO BED WITHOUT READING MY BIBLE. WOULD YOU?

OH BROTHER! COME ON, LET'S GO!

THE ADVENTURES OF...

JEREMIAH

by ©1988
H-12

JEREMIAH IS BEING TEMPTED WITH MONEY FROM THE CHURCH SAFE.

COME ON, JEREMIAH... LET'S TAKE A LITTLE OF THIS MONEY.

BUT...

NOBODY WILL EVER MISS IT.

IT'S NOT EVEN COUNTED YET.

BUT...

THEY'LL PROBABLY FIGURE IT WAS JUST A LIGHT SUNDAY.

BUT...

AND YOU'LL BE ABLE TO BUY THAT CD PLAYER YOU'VE ALWAYS WANTED.

BUT...

LOOK AT IT THIS WAY. THIS IS A SMALL PAYMENT FOR ALL THE HOURS OF SERVICE YOU'VE PUT INTO BUILDING THIS CHURCH.

BUT...

COME ON, JEREMIAH. WHAT DO YOU SAY?

THE ADVENTURES OF...

JEREMIAH

by ©1988 Jay Wheeler H-14

IN TRYING TO SNEAK THE STOLEN OFFERING BACK INTO THE CHURCH OFFICE, JEREMIAH AND MATT ARE CAUGHT BY A NEW BURGLAR ALARM SYSTEM.

RRRRR
OH NO!
CLANG CLANG

RRRRRR
CLANG CLANG
WHOOP WHOOP

LET'S RUN FOR IT, JEREMIAH.

NO LET'S JUST WAIT HERE FOR THE POLICE TO ARRIVE.

WHAT? ARE YOU CRAZY?

I WOULD BE IF I RAN AWAY.

HUH?

I DON'T THINK I'D BE ABLE TO LIVE WITH MYSELF ANY EASIER IF I RAN AWAY FROM THIS...

...THAN IF I HAD KEPT THE MONEY.

OH BROTHER! REMIND ME NOT TO INVITE YOU ON MY NEXT PRANK.

DON'T WORRY.

THE POLICE SOON ARRIVED AND OUR CRIMINALS WERE HAULED OFF TO JAIL.

GIVE ME YOUR WORST! I DESERVE IT!

AND THE WORST IS WHAT THEY GOT!

THEIR CHURCH, BELIEVING THAT THEY WERE RESPONSIBLE FOR OTHER DISAPPEARANCES, FILED CHARGES AGAINST THEM.

ON TOP OF THAT, THEIR FRIENDS NO LONGER WANTED TO HAVE ANYTHING TO DO WITH THEM.

AND IT GOT WORSE! GRAMPS, UNDER THE STRESS OF DISAPPOINTMENT, HAD A MASSIVE HEART ATTACK.

PLUS, JEREMIAH'S DOG DIED.

WAKE UP! YOU'RE SLEEPING IN CHURCH. HERE'S THE OFFERING PLATE! PASS IT DOWN.

IT WOULD BE KIND OF FUN TO TAKE SOME MONEY OUT INSTEAD OF PUT IT IN FOR A CHANGE, EH?

THE ADVENTURES OF... JEREMIAH

by ©1989 Ron Wheeler I-1

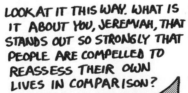

TO BE CONTINUED ...

THE ADVENTURES OF...

JEREMIAH

by ©1989
Wheeler
I-3

JEREMIAH FEELS AWFUL THE MORNING AFTER CHIP'S PARTY.

GRAMPS, I FEEL SICK TO MY STOMACH!

JEREMIAH, WHAT DID YOU DO TO MAKE YOURSELF SICK?

I FEEL SICK BECAUSE I DID SOMETHING I KNEW WAS WRONG LAST NIGHT.

I... WATCHED SOME VIDEOS!

VIDEOS?

SOME OF WHAT THEY CALL "QUESTIONABLE" VIDEOS.

...ALTHOUGH THERE WAS NOTHING QUESTIONABLE ABOUT THEM.

THEY WERE VILE DISGUST-ING FILMS.

THE ADVENTURES OF...

JEREMIAH

by ©1989 Roy Wheeler I-4

MATT SPOTS JEREMIAH IN THE HALLWAY

SEE YOU LATER, CHIP.

JEREMIAH?

HI, MATT.

WERE YOU JUST TALKING WITH CHIP?

SURE!

AFTER SNUBBING YOU IN CLASS AND SUBJECTING YOU TO THOSE DISGUSTING VIDEOS AT HIS HOUSE, YOU STILL WANT TO SPEAK TO HIM AGAIN?

HEY, HE'S NOT SUCH A BAD GUY, MATT. YOU HAVE TO EXPECT THAT WHEN PEOPLE ARE LOST.

I'D LIKE TO TELL HIM TO GET LOST.

GRAMPS GAVE ME A NEW PERSPECTIVE ON HOW TO REACH THE WORLD FOR JESUS.

INSTEAD OF WITNESSING IN GROUP SITUATIONS WHERE PEOPLE MIGHT TEASE US OR SNUB US...

THE ADVENTURES OF...

JEREMIAH

by ©1989
Wheeler
I-26

LUKE AND JEREMIAH ARE PLAYING FRISBEE AT BENTON PARK.

GREAT CATCH, LUKE.

OOMPF!

YOU OKAY, LUKE?

JEREMIAH, COME HERE! QUICK!

LOOK WHAT I FOUND!

SO? IT'S A BUNCH OF OLD MAGAZINES.

THESE AREN'T JUST ANY MAGAZINES.

THE ADVENTURES OF...

JEREMIAH

by ©1989
Wheeler
I-27

LUKE AND JEREMIAH DISCOVERED SOME DIRTY MAGAZINES AT BENTON PARK.

IT'S A GOOD THING WE THREW THOSE MAGAZINES AWAY ISN'T IT, JEREMIAH?

IT SURE IS.

I'M GLAD WE DIDN'T LOOK AT THEM MUCH.

YEAH, WELL TRY NOT TO THINK ABOUT THEM, LUKE.

YOU KNOW, I CAN'T IMAGINE HAVING MAGAZINES LIKE THAT AROUND OUR HOUSE.

ME NEITHER. DON'T THINK ABOUT IT, LUKE.

NICE DAY OUT, HUH?

YES IT IS.

TO BE CONTINUED...

THE ADVENTURES OF...

JEREMIAH

by © 1999
Ron Wheeler
I-28

LUKE CAN'T GET HIS MIND OFF OF THOSE DIRTY MAGAZINES.

I CAN'T BELIEVE I LOOKED AT THOSE MAGAZINES.

I MEAN THAT WAS REALLY SOME RAUNCHY JUNK.

I ONLY LOOKED AT A COUPLE OF THEM. I WONDER WHAT WAS IN THE OTHER MAGAZINES.

PROBABLY MORE OF THE SAME GARBAGE.

STILL ... THERE MIGHT BE SOMETHING EVEN MORE "INTERESTING" IN THOSE.

I WONDER IF THOSE MAGAZINES ARE STILL IN THE PARK.

WHAT AM I SAYING? I CAN'T GO BACK THERE. IT'S THE MIDDLE OF THE NIGHT!

BUT WHAT BETTER TIME TO GO BACK IF YOU DON'T WANT ANYONE TO SEE YOU!

WAIT A MINUTE! THIS IS WRONG! THAT JUNK IS GARBAGE! IT'LL WARP MY MIND! MY FACE WILL BREAK OUT! I'LL GROW HAIR ON MY PALMS!

AND I'M GOING TO LAY HERE ALL NIGHT WRESTLING WITH THIS IN MY MIND.

I NEED TO DISTRACT MYSELF WITH SOME- THING... ANYTHING!

WHAT'S THIS HAVE TO SAY?

"FINALLY BROTHERS, WHATEVER IS TRUE, WHATEVER IS NOBLE, WHATEVER IS RIGHT, WHATEVER IS PURE, WHATEVER IS LOVELY, WHATEVER IS ADMIRABLE, - IF ANYTHING IS EXCELLENT OR PRAISEWORTHY- THINK ABOUT SUCH THINGS."

WELL THAT CLEARLY EXCLUDES PORNOGRAPHY. THE ONLY THING LEFT TO THINK ABOUT IS...

...A NOBLE HOT FUDGE SUNDAE.

THE ADVENTURES OF...
JEREMIAH
by Wheeler
I-29

MATT AND LUKE ARE PLAYING WITH A NERF BALL.

OKAY, WHAT'LL YOU GIVE ME IF I MAKE THIS SHOT?

MY HEARTY CONGRATULATIONS.

COME ON, MAKE IT WORTH MY TIME. GIVE ME SOME INCENTIVE IF I MAKE IT. GIVE ME A QUARTER.

FORGET IT!

OKAY, WATCH THIS!

YOU MADE IT!

I CAN'T BELIEVE IT!

PURE TALENT!

I'LL BET YOU CAN'T DO THAT TWICE IN A ROW.

OH REALLY? HOW MUCH DO YOU WANT TO BET?

JUST THROW THE BALL.

NO, COME ON! HOW MUCH DO YOU WANT TO BET, BIG SHOT?

TO BE CONTINUED...

THE ADVENTURES OF...

JEREMIAH

by ©1990 Ron Wheeler I-31

LUKE FINDS HIMSELF WITH A HUGE GAMBLING DEBT.

YOU GAMBLED AWAY THE HOUSE?

YEAH, I GUESS I SORT OF OVERDID IT, DIDN'T I?

WHAT AM I GOING TO DO, PENNY?

WAIT A MINUTE, LUKE, LET ME GET A FEW THINGS STRAIGHT.

FIRST OF ALL, THE HOUSE ISN'T YOURS TO GAMBLE.

IT ISN'T?

NO, IT BELONGS TO OUR PARENTS.

YOU CAN'T GAMBLE AWAY SOMETHING THAT DOESN'T BELONG TO YOU.

I CAN'T?

AND SECOND, YOU'RE A MINOR. GAMBLING IS ILLEGAL FOR MINORS.

IT IS?

TO BE CONTINUED...

THE ADVENTURES OF...

JEREMIAH

by ©1990
Wheeler
I-32

MATT TRIES TO COLLECT HIS GAMBLING DEBT.

COME ON, YOU GUYS, PACK IT UP! GET OUT OF HERE! THIS IS MY HOUSE NOW!

MATT, YOU DON'T REALLY EXPECT TO COLLECT ON THIS DEBT, DO YOU?

HEY, I WON IT FAIR AND SQUARE.

I WAS WILLING TO STOP AT $50,000, BUT NO! LUKE SAYS, DOUBLE OR NOTHING! I'LL GIVE YOU MY HOUSE IF I LOSE!

YOU WANT ME TO WALK AWAY FROM THIS THING JUST BECAUSE YOU DON'T REALLY EXPECT ME TO COLLECT ON IT?

YES!

FORGET IT!

I TELL YOU WHAT, LUKE, INSTEAD OF THE HOUSE, YOU CAN MOW MY LAWN EVERY WEEK AT $3.50 PER HOUR UNTIL YOU PAY IT OFF.

NO, MATT.

* LUKE 7:41,42

THE ADVENTURES OF... JEREMIAH

by ©1990 Ray Wheeler I-41

JEREMIAH MUST LIVE WITH THE FACT THAT NOBODY SAW HIM DONATE $50 FOR A NEEDY CAUSE.

I WANT TO REPORT TO YOU GUYS THAT YOUR RESPONSE TO OUR FUND DRIVE WAS EXCELLENT.

WE HAVE MORE THAN ENOUGH TO BUY JASON A NEW RADIO.

OH BOY! THAT'S GREAT!

I'M ALSO PLEASED TO TELL YOU THAT MOST OF THE MONEY CAME FROM ONE GENEROUS INDIVIDUAL...

WAS THAT YOU, LUKE?

...WHO I'M SURE WISHES TO REMAIN ANONYMOUS.

THAT'S OKAY, LUKE, YOU DON'T HAVE TO SAY ANYTHING. WE KNOW.

I.... UH...

WAY TO GO, LUKE.

ATTA BOY, LUKE.

YOU OLE SOFTY.

I...UH...

HEY, EVERYBODY, I THINK WE SHOULD GIVE LUKE THE JOB OF DELIVERING THE RADIO TO JASON.

THE ADVENTURES OF... JEREMIAH

by © 1990 Roy Wheeler I-42

GRAMPS EXPLAINS SOME SPIRITUAL PRINCIPALS

IN MATTHEW SIX, JESUS SAYS, "(VS 3) BUT WHEN YOU GIVE TO THE NEEDY, DO NOT LET YOUR LEFT HAND KNOW WHAT YOUR RIGHT HAND IS DOING."

"(VS 4) SO THAT YOUR GIVING MAY BE IN SECRET. THEN YOUR FATHER WHO SEES WHAT IS DONE IN SECRET, WILL REWARD YOU."

HMMM.

YOUR HUMAN TENDENCY IS TO WANT EVERYONE TO KNOW WHEN YOU DO SOMETHING NICE...

LIKE HELP TO BUY A RADIO FOR A SICK KID, HUH?

...ESPECIALLY IF IT'S SACRIFICIAL.

AS IN $50 BUCKS SACRIFICIAL?

...AND ESPECIALLY IF EVERYONE THINKS YOU DID NOTHING.

LIKE MY WHOLE SUNDAY SCHOOL CLASS DOES?

BUT GOD SAYS HE WILL REWARD US.

BUT HOW?

TO BE CONTINUED...

THE ADVENTURES OF...

JEREMIAH

by ©1990
Ron Wheeler
I-43

LUKE GIVES JEREMIAH THE HONOR OF DELIVERING THE RADIO TO JASON.

HEY, LUKE, WHY DON'T YOU COME WITH ME?

HUH?

I DON'T DESERVE TO. I GOT ALL THOSE PATS ON THE BACK FOR BEING THE BIG CONTRIBUTOR TO THIS THING.

YET I ONLY PITCHED IN A COUPLE BUCKS.

THAT DOESN'T MATTER.

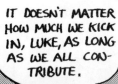

IT DOESN'T MATTER HOW MUCH WE KICK IN, LUKE, AS LONG AS WE ALL CONTRIBUTE.

BUT I THOUGHT YOU DIDN'T GIVE ANYTHING.

UH...

WAIT A MINUTE. I SAW YOU GO BACK INTO THE CLASSROOM LATER ON. IS THAT WHEN YOU PUT YOUR MONEY IN?

WE'D BETTER GET GOING, LUKE.

THE ADVENTURES OF...

JEREMIAH

by ©1991 Tom Wheeler K-45

TO BE CONTINUED...

THE ADVENTURES OF... JEREMIAH

by ©1991 Ron Wheeler K-46

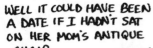

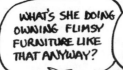

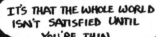

THE ADVENTURES OF...

JEREMIAH

by ©1991
Roy Wheeler
K-47

Luke agrees to go on a diet.

OKAY! OKAY! YOU'VE CONVINCED ME! THAT'S ENOUGH!

...AND 1COR. 3:16 SAYS, "DON'T YOU KNOW THAT YOU YOURSELVES ARE GOD'S TEMPLE AND THAT GOD'S SPIRIT LIVES IN YOU?"

I WILL GO ON A DIET.

YEA!

YOU KNOW IT FEELS GOOD TO FINALLY GIVE SOMETHING OVER TO THE LORD THAT YOU'VE BEEN CLINGING TO FOR SO LONG.

Luke dove into his diet with fervor.

NO FRENCH FRIES FOR ME. I'LL STICK WITH THESE CARROT STICKS.

BUT AFTER HE LOST A COUPLE OF POUNDS...

HEY, I'M MAKING PROGRESS, I THINK I'LL REWARD MYSELF WITH THIS LITTLE PIECE OF CAKE.

...HE BEGAN TO RATIONALIZE... THAT IS, HE MADE RATIONAL LIES ABOUT HIS EATING.

I'M REALLY STARVING! A FEW OF THESE TINY COOKIES TO CURB MY APPETITE CAN'T HURT MUCH.

MUNCH MUNCH

THE ADVENTURES OF...

JEREMIAH

by ©1991
Roy Wheeler
K-48

Luke hits rock bottom with his food addiction.

5¢

WILL WORK FOR TWINKIES

LUKE! THERE YOU ARE!

GO AWAY, SIS! I'M NO GOOD!

COME ON HOME WITH US, LUKE.

WE'LL GET YOU SOME PROFESSIONAL HELP.

Luke did get some professional help.

He joined a weight-loss program to help him learn how to eat right.

He visited with counselors to help him learn more about how he was rationalizing his overeating.

HMMM

...And he dug into the word to learn how much God loved him.

"FOR HE SATISFIES THE THIRSTY AND FILLS THE HUNGRY WITH GOOD THINGS."*

THE ADVENTURES OF...

JEREMIAH

by Ron Wheeler
© 1991
L-1

Matt shows off something new.

GUESS WHAT I'VE GOT, LUKE?

WELL, I CAN SEE IT ISN'T A NEW FACE. YOU'VE STILL GOT THE SAME OLD UGLY ONE.

NO, STUPID, CHECK OUT THE SUSPENDERS.

NICE.

NICE? THESE HAPPEN TO BE AUTHENTIC PIERRE KLEIN DESIGNER SUSPENDERS.

SO?

SO? EVERYBODY WHO'S ANYBODY IS WEARING PIERRE KLEIN SUSPENDERS.

OH, GO ON.

LOOK AROUND YOU. ALL THE COOL PEOPLE HAVE THEM. IF YOU AREN'T WEARING THEM, YOU JUST AREN'T COOL.

COOL?

YOU'D BETTER GET A PAIR. OTHERWISE YOU RISK ETERNAL SLIMEDOM.

ETERNAL SLIMEDOM?

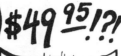

THE ADVENTURES OF...

JEREMIAH

by ©1991
Rod Wheeler
L-2

MATT AND LUKE'S PIERRE KLEIN SUSPENDERS WERE A BIG HIT.

EVERYONE WHO WANTED TO BE COOL BOUGHT A PAIR.

ONE AT A TIME, FOLKS.

HURRY WHILE THEY LAST.

SOME PEOPLE EVEN RESORTED TO MANIPULATION TO GET A PAIR.

DADDY, YOU WANT ME TO BE POPULAR IN SCHOOL, DON'T YOU?

HMMM...

EVERYONE WHO'S POPULAR IS WEARING PIERRE KLEIN DESIGNER SUSPENDERS. CAN I HAVE A PAIR?

SURE, I GUESS SO. HOW MUCH?

ONLY $68.95.

$68.95? I'VE GOT A TEN DOLLAR PAIR IN MY CLOSET. WHY DON'T YOU WEAR THOSE!

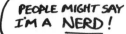

THE ADVENTURES OF...

JEREMIAH

by ©1992 Roy Wheeler L-10

ON A NICE DAY, THE GANG PLAYS A LITTLE FRISBEE.

CATCH THIS ONE, MATT.

I GOT IT! I GOT IT!

CRASH

HE GOT IT ALL RIGHT.

CAN'T YOU WATCH WHERE YOU'RE GOING, YOU STUPID SCUM-SUCKER!

GASP!

LUKE, DID YOU SAY WHAT I THOUGHT YOU SAID?

NO, THAT WASN'T ME. THAT WAS SOME GUY DOWN THE STREET.

LUKE, DON'T LIE.

THE ADVENTURES OF...

JEREMIAH

by ©1992
Roy Wheeler
L-11

Luke feels terrible for his language problem.

Luke, that's no way to solve your problem.

Your problem isn't with your mouth. It's with your heart.

For out of the overflow of his heart his mouth speaks. *

* LUKE 6:45

Let's just take this tape off.

YEEOOWW!

RIP!

You almost ripped my lips off, you stupid scum-sucker!

GASP!

He said it again!

Maybe we DO need to tape your mouth, Luke!

Scum-sucker! Scum-sucker! Scum-sucker!

*EPHESIANS 4:29

*JOSHUA 1:8

THE ADVENTURES OF...

JEREMIAH

by ©1992
Roy Wheeler
L-29

PENNY IS WALKING WITH A LIMP.

WHAT'S WRONG WITH YOU?

OH, I STUBBED MY TOE AWHILE BACK AND NOW I THINK THE NAIL IS STARTING TO FALL OFF.

UGH!

SEE?

NO I DON'T WANT TO LOOK!

WHY NOT?

THREE REASONS!

NUMBER ONE...I DON'T WANT YOUR SMELLY FEET IN MY FACE.

MY FEET DON'T SMELL.

NUMBER TWO...I ESPECIALLY DON'T WANT A SMELLY FOOT WITH AN ABNORMAL GROWTH ON IT IN MY FACE.

IT'S NOT...

TO BE CONTINUED...

THE ADVENTURES OF...

JEREMIAH

by ©1992
R. Wheeler
L-48

ON AN AVERAGE EVENING ALL ACROSS AMERICA LITTLE BLUE LIGHTS GLOW FROM NEARLY EVERY HOME.

UPON CLOSER EXAMINATION WE FIND RESIDENTS OF ALL AGES FOCUSED ON A LIGHT AND SOUND EMITTING LITTLE BOX DISPLAYED PROMINENTLY IN THE MAIN ROOM OF THE HOUSE.

ALL EYES ARE RIVETED ON THE BOX... NO CONVERSATION OCCURS ... NO MOVEMENT IS MADE ... NO EYES BLINK ... NO THINKING IS DONE ... OCCUPANTS FALL INTO A TRANCE-LIKE CONCENTRATION ON THE BOX.

OCCASIONALLY THE CHIEF RESIDENT OF THE DOMICILE PRETENDS TO HAVE SOME SEMBLANCE OF CONTROL OVER THE BOX AS HE CLICKS A SMALL DEVICE AT IT PERIODICALLY.

CLICK
CLICK

BUT THIS IS TO NO AVAIL. THE GLOWING BOX MERELY CHANGES ITS SOUND AND COLOR IMAGES. IT STILL MAINTAINS ITS DEATH GRIP ON THE RESIDENTS.

MEANWHILE, BOOKS COLLECT DUST... SPORTS EQUIPMENT REMAIN UNUSED... CHORES GO UNDONE... PETS ARE IGNORED... MANY FACETS OF LIFE SHUT DOWN.

SIGH

NIGHT AFTER NIGHT THE CATATONIC RITUAL GOES ON. GRADUALLY THE MESSAGES EMANATING FROM THE BOX TAKE ON A DARKER AND DARKER TONE.

SEX! VIOLENCE! PROFANITY! VULGARITY! YUCK!

WHAT WAS ONCE PERSONAL AND PRIVATE BECOMES PUBLIC. WHAT WAS ONCE SHOCKING BECOMES NORMAL. WHAT WAS ONCE NORMAL IS NOW PORTRAYED AS STRANGE.

GRADUALLY... GRADUALLY... THE DEEP SEATED VALUES OF THE POPULACE BEGIN TO SHIFT. WHAT WAS RIGHT IS NOW WRONG... AND WHAT WAS WRONG IS NOW RIGHT.

RIGHT WRONG

BOY, THIS BOOK IS TOO SCARY. I THINK I'M GOING TO GO WATCH TV FOR AWHILE.

TV'S EFFECTS

THE ADVENTURES OF...

JEREMIAH

by ©1993
BWheeler
M-16

MATT DECIDES HE DOESN'T LIKE BEING A CHRISTIAN ANY MORE.

GASP! WHAT DID YOU SAY?

I JUST SAID IT'S NO FUN BEING A CHRISTIAN

THERE'S ALL OF THESE EXCITING THINGS OUT THERE THAT I CAN'T DO BECAUSE OF WHAT I'VE CHOSEN TO BE.

I MEAN AREN'T YOU EVEN A LITTLE BIT CURIOUS ABOUT HOW THE OTHER SIDE LIVES?

WOULDN'T YOU LIKE TO JUST TAKE A DAY OFF FROM BEING A GOODY GOODY AND LIVE IT UP A LITTLE?

WOULDN'T YOU LIKE TO GO OUT AND JUST...

HOLD IT!

NO! I LOVE CHRIST TOO MUCH FOR WHAT HE DID FOR ME TO WILLINGLY GO OUT AND DO THAT.

* JOHN 8:31, 32

THE ADVENTURES OF...

JEREMIAH

by ©1993
Ron Wheeler
M-17

MATT DECIDES HE WANTS TO LIVE A SINFUL LIFE.

LET'S SEE, THERE'S NO LISTING OF SIN IN THE YELLOW PAGES.

HOW AM I GOING TO FIND OUT EXACTLY HOW THE OTHER HALF LIVES IF I DON'T EVEN KNOW WHERE TO GO TO FIND IT?

ΣΩΥ FRATERNITY

PARTY

EXCUSE ME DO YOU KNOW WHERE I CAN FIND A SINFUL LIFE?

SAY WHAT?

YOU'RE IN A COLLEGE FRATERNITY. YOU SHOULD KNOW ALL ABOUT SIN. CAN YOU GIVE ME SOME DIRECTION?

WHAT?

YEAH! THIS WAY!

?

BOOT!

THE ADVENTURES OF...

JEREMIAH

by ©1993
Ron Wheeler
M-19

LUKE HAS MADE A MAJOR DECISION.

WHAT'S YOUR MAJOR DECISION, LUKE?

I HAVE REACHED A MILESTONE, JEREMIAH.

I HAVE DECIDED THAT I NO LONGER NEED GIRLS IN MY LIFE.

YOU WHAT?

I DON'T NEED GIRLS.

OH REALLY!

I MEAN, MY MOM'S OKAY, AND I SUPPOSE I'LL LET MY SISTER TALK TO ME FROM TIME TO TIME.

BUT GENERALLY, I HAVE VERY LITTLE USE FOR THE FEMALE GENDER.

SO WHAT BROUGHT THIS ON?

NOTHING... I JUST DECIDED TO NO LONGER BE A VICTIM OF MY RAGING ADOLESCENT HORMONES...

TO BE CONTINUED...

THE ADVENTURES OF...

JEREMIAH

by ©1993
Ron Wheeler
M-21

AFTER SEVERAL GIRLS EXPRESS THEIR DISPLEASURE TOWARD LUKE, HE OPENS UP TO JEREMIAH.

IT'S ABOUT TIME.

SIGH! OKAY, I'LL TELL YOU WHAT HAPPENED.

AWHILE BACK I WAS REALLY YEARNING FOR A SPECIAL RELATIONSHIP WITH A GIRL ... LIKE YOU HAVE WITH TRUDY.

YEAH?

AND I THOUGHT...WHERE CAN I MEET SOME CUTE ENERGETIC YOUNG FEMALE THAT CAN FILL THAT NEED.

YEAH?

THATS WHEN I DECIDED TO BE THE BEAUTY PAGEANT JUDGE.

BEAUTY PAGEANT? WHAT BEAUTY PAGEANT?

"THE GREATER AREA MISS VIVACIOUS CONTEST."

MISS VIVACIOUS CONTEST?

HOW DID YOU GET TO BE A JUDGE FOR SOMETHING LIKE THAT?

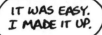

THE ADVENTURES OF...

JEREMIAH

by ©1993
Wheder
M-5

JEREMIAH IS DRIVING MATT.

SO, GRANDMA, LET'S GET GOING.

WHY ARE YOU DRIVING SO SLOW?

THE POSTED SPEED LIMIT IS ONLY 35 MILES PER HOUR.

YEAH, BUT THAT'S WHEN YOU'RE MOVING FORWARD.

YOU'RE DRIVING SO SLOW WE'RE GOING IN REVERSE.

WE'LL GET THERE OKAY.

BUT WHAT GIVES? WE'RE SUPPOSED TO GET THERE THIS AFTERNOON, NOT NEXT WEEK.

WE'LL BE LATE.

BETTER TO ARRIVE SAFELY THAN NOT AT ALL.

OH, WELL THANK YOU, SERGEANT SAFETY. WHAT HAPPENED? DID YOU JUST SEE A DRIVER'S ED. TRAINING FILM?

THE ADVENTURES OF...

JEREMIAH

by ©1993
Tom Wheeler
M-6

JEREMIAH AND MATT STOP TO PICK UP LUKE.

LET'S HURRY, JEREMIAH. I HAVEN'T GOT A LOT OF TIME.

WELL, THEN YOU MIGHT WANT TO HITCH A RIDE ON A PASSING SNAIL.

WHAT DO YOU MEAN? WHY AREN'T WE MOVING?

WE ARE MOVING. THIS IS AS FAST AS OLD SPEED KING WILL GO.

WHAT GIVES, JEREMIAH?

I'VE GOT MY HANDS POSITIONED AT 10 AND 2 O'CLOCK. I GLANCE INTO MY MIRRORS EVERY SIX SECONDS.

MY SEAT BELT IS SECURELY FASTENED.

WHAT IS HE DOING?

HE'S BEING CAUTIOUS. HE JUST FOUND OUT HOW MUCH HIS DAD IS PAYING EXTRA FOR HIS AUTO INSURANCE.

THE ADVENTURES OF...

JEREMIAH

by ©1993
Wheeler
M-7

JEREMIAH FORGOT ABOUT A HOMEWORK ASSIGNMENT AND SPEEDS TO GET HOME.

SLOW DOWN JEREMIAH!

YOU'LL GET US ALL KILLED!

ZOOOM

I CAN'T! MY PAPER ON SELF-CONTROL IS DUE TOMORROW AND I HAVEN'T EVEN STARTED YET.

SELF-CONTROL? YOU'RE WRITING A PAPER ON SELF-CONTROL? YOU SHOULD CALL IT "OUT OF CONTROL"

I'VE GOT TO HURRY!

BUT WHAT ABOUT BEING CAUTIOUS BECAUSE OF YOUR DAD'S HIGH INSURANCE RATES?

HUH?

YOU KNOW, YOU'RE RIGHT. I'D BETTER SLOW DOWN.

SCREEE

THE ADVENTURES OF...

JEREMIAH

by ©1993
Tony
Wheeler
M-9

JEREMIAH WASN'T PAYING ATTENTION AND RAN INTO A TREE.

DAD, ARE YOU SITTING DOWN?

SAY, YOU KNOW THOSE HIGH CAR INSURANCE RATES WE WERE TALKING ABOUT BECAUSE I'M A HIGH RISK TEENAGER?

WELL, I DECIDED THOSE INSURANCE COMPANIES KNOW WHAT THEY'RE DOING.

YEAH, I HAD A SLIGHT ACCIDENT. NO, NO-ONE WAS HURT.

WELL ACTUALLY, I RAN INTO A TREE ... BUT IT WASN'T MY FAULT.

I MEAN IT JUMPED OUT IN FRONT OF MY CAR.

THE ADVENTURES OF...

JEREMIAH

by ©1993
Ron Wheeler
M-33

LUKE AND JEREMIAH GET TURNED AWAY AT THE BALLPARK.

OH NO! IT'S SOLD OUT! RATS!

TICKETS

SOLD OUT!

OH WELL, I GUESS WE'LL HAVE TO DO SOMETHING ELSE TODAY.

THIS MAKES ME SO ANGRY!

I WAS LOOKING FORWARD TO THIS GAME FOR SO LONG AND NOW WE CAN'T GET IN.

OH WELL.

WHY? WHY? WHY? IT'S NOT FAIR I TELL YOU! IT'S NOT FAIR!

STOMP STOMP STOMP

PANT PANT

ARE YOU THROUGH?

YEAH, WHY AREN'T YOU UPSET, JEREMIAH?

I DON'T KNOW.

*JAMES 1:2

TO BE CONTINUED...

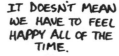